Warren Hastings

A Letter from Warren Hastings, Esq., Dated 21st of February,

1784

With remarks and authentic documents to support the remarks

Warren Hastings

A Letter from Warren Hastings, Esq., Dated 21st of February, 1784
With remarks and authentic documents to support the remarks

ISBN/EAN: 9783337012762

Printed in Europe, USA, Canada, Australia, Japan

Cover: Foto ©ninafisch / pixelio.de

More available books at **www.hansebooks.com**

A
LETTER

FROM

WARREN HASTINGS, Esq.

DATED 21st of FEBRUARY, 1784.

WITH

REMARKS

AND

AUTHENTIC DOCUMENTS

TO SUPPORT THE REMARKS.

LONDON:

PRINTED FOR JAMES RIDGWAY, OPPOSITE
SACKVILLE-STREET, PICCADILLY.
MDCCLXXXVI.

PREFACE.

IF the report was true, that Mr. Haftings had applied to be re-appointed to the Government of Bengal, a direct negative to fuch an application, might have been fairly founded on his own declarations, contained in the Letter now printed, viz. that age and infirmity had not only impaired his conftitution, but his faculties.

Another

Another report is ftill in circula-
tion, and generally believed, that
he, or his friends have applied for
a penfion for him to the Court of
Directors of the Eaft India Company,
and that the Directors have it in
contemplation to give him five thoufand pounds a year. The plea made
in his behalf is long and able fervices
and great poverty. Before the Directors take their refolution, a Letter
from himfelf, materially connected
with fuch a plea, and the Remarks
upon it, are publickly brought into
their view, and recommended to
their previous confideration.

The

The prefent publication is not meant to injure Mr. Haftings, unlefs it be deemed an injury to prevent his receiving a gratuity to which he has no juft claim, nor even an equitable pretenfion.

TO THE HONOURABLE

COURT of DIRECTORS, &c.

On the River Ganges, Feb. 21, 1784.

HONOURABLE SIRS,

HAVING had occasion to disburse from my own cash many sums for services, which, though required to enable me to execute the duties of my station, I have hitherto omitted to enter in my public accounts, and my own fortune being unequal to so heavy a charge, I have resolved to reimburse my-self *in a mode the most suitable to your affairs,* by charging the same in my Durbar accounts of the present year, and crediting them by a sum *privately received,* and appropriated to your service in the same manner as other

B   sums

fums received on account of the Honourable Company, and already carried to their account.

The particulars of thefe difburfements are contained in the enclofed accounts No. 1, 2, 3 and 4, of which No. 5 is the abftract. I fhall fubjoin a brief explanation of each.

The fum of the account No. 1 is the difference between the allowance of 300 rupees per month, which was the cuftomary pay of the Governor's Military Secretary, and that which I allowed to Lieutenant Colonel Ironfide, during the time he acted in that capacity, on account of his fuperior rank. It was referred to your Honourable Court in one of the letters of the year 1773 or 4; but I prefume that it was overlooked in the preffure of other more important matters, which at that time occupied your attention.

No. 2 and 3 are explained in the accounts themfelves. No. 4 confifts of three feveral kinds

kinds of charges, which I confefs to have been unauthorized, but which I humbly conceive neither to be of a private nature, nor unworthy fubjects of the bounty of a great and rifing ftate. The firft is inconfiderable, confifting chiefly in the fubfiftence of the Pundits, who were affembled in Calcutta, and employed during two years in compiling the code of Hindoo laws for your ufe, the fum allotted to them was one rupee *per diem.* A larger recompence was offered, but refufed; nor would they receive this, but for their daily fupport. They had indeed the promife of fome public endowments for their colleges, which yet remains unperformed. The fecond is the amount of fundry monthly falaries paid to fome of the moft learned profeffors of the Mahomedan law for tranflating from the Arabic into the Perfian tongue a compendium of their law called the Hedaya, which is held in high eftimation and part of a more voluminous work, which I could not profecute. Your Honourable Court is in pof-

B 2   feffion

session of a part of the English version of
the Hedaya made by Mr. James Anderson,
and the subsequent part of the same book
has been lately translated by Mr. Hamilton.
These gentlemen are both engaged in the
completion, and are both eminently quali-
fied for it. It would exceed the bounds of
this letter to expatiate on the utility of this
work; yet I may be allowed to vindicate
the expence of it by one summary argument,
which is that, while the Mahomedan law
is allowed to be the standard of the criminal
jurisprudence of your dominions under the
control and inspection of your English servants, it seems indispensably necessary that
the Judges of the courts should have a
more familiar guide for their proceedings
than the books of the Arabic tongue, of
which few have opportunities of attaining
a competent knowledge, and as necessary
that your servants should possess the means
of consulting the principles, on which those
judgments are founded, which, in their
ultimate resort and in extraordinary cases,

may

may fall within their immediate cogni-
zance, and of the laws, of which they are
the protectors. The third charge is that
of an academy inftituted for the ftudy of
the different branches of fciences taught in
the Mahomedan fchools. After a trial of
about two years, finding that it was likely
to anfwer the end of its inftitution, I recommended to the Board and obtained their
confent to pafs the fubfequent expence of
the eftablifhment to the account of the
Company and to erect a building for the
purpofe at *my own* immediate coft, but
for a Company's interefted note *granted
me for the reimburfement of it.* It is almoft
the only complete eftablifhment of the
kind now exifting in India, although they
were once in univerfal ufe, and the decayed remains of thefe fchools are yet to be
feen in every capital town and city of Hin-
doftan and Decan. It has contributed to
extend the credit of the Company's name,
and to foften the prejudices excited by the
rapid growth of the Britifh dominion, and
it

it is a feminary of the moft ufeful members of fociety. I humbly fubmit the
propriety of carrying thefe expences to
your account by the confideration, that it
was not poffible for me to have been influenced in incurring them by any purpofe
of my own intereft. Something perhaps
may be attributed to the impulfe of pride in
the fhare, which I might hope to derive of
a public benefaction ; but certainly not to
vanity or oftentation ; fince I believe it to
be generally conceived that the whole expence, of which the greateft part is yet
my own, has been already defrayed from
the Treafury of the Company.

I will candidly confefs that, when I firft
engaged both in this and the preceding expences, I had no intention of carrying it to
the account of the Company. Improvident for myfelf, zealous for the honour of
my country, and the credit and interefts of
my employers, I feldom permitted my
Profpects of futurity to enter into the views
of

of my private concerns. In the undisturbed exercise of the faculties, which appertain to the active season of my life, I confined all my regards to my public character, and reckoned on a fund of years to come for its duration. The infirmities of life have since succeeded, and I have lately received more than one severe warning to retire from a scene, to which my bodily strength is no longer equal, and threatens me with a corresponding decay in whatever powers of mind I once possessed to discharge the laborious duties and hard vicissitudes of my station. With this change in my condition, I am compelled to depart from that liberal plan, which I originally adopted, and to claim from your justice, for you have forbad me to appeal to your generosity, the discharge of a debt, which I can, with the most scrupulous integrity, aver to be justly my due, and which I cannot sustain. If it should be objected, that the allowance of these demands would furnish a precedent for others of the like kind, I have to remark

mark that, in their whole amount, they are but the aggregate of a contingent account of twelve years ; and, if it were to become the practice of thofe, who have paffed their prime of life in your fervice, and filled, fo long as I have filled it, the firft office of your dominion, to glean from their paft accounts all the little articles of expence, which their inaccuracy or indifference hath overlooked, your intereft would fuffer infinitely lefs by the precedent, than by a fingle example of a life fpent *in the accumulation of crores* for your benefit, and doomed in its clofe *to fuffer the extremities of private want and fink in obfcurity !*

I have thought it proper to complete the prefent fubject by the addition of a charge, which I intended to have fubmitted to the board, but which, if divided at this time from the others, might have admitted an unfair conftruction. It is in the account No. 6, and confifts of charges incurred for boats and budgerows provided by me, for my

own

own ufe, on fuch public occafions, as required my departure from the Prefidency on
extraordinary fervices.

My predeceffors have always had an eftablifhment of this kind provided for them,
and my fucceffor will have a provifion de-
volve to him *fuperior in convenience and in
elegance to any that I have yet feen,* and furnifhed with a coft, which could not be credited by thofe, who have feen the fubjects
of it.

I have the honour, &c.

Your's, &c.

(Signed)   WARREN HASTINGS.

C   *Heads*

Heads of the Account enclosed in the preceding Letter.

1. Salary to Col. Ironside while acting as the Governor's Military Secretary from April 1772 to May 1773, - - - -   8,511 7 6
2. Charges in the Governor General's office from Sept. 1772 to 1st Jan. 1774, - - - - - - -   1,49,870 11 9
3. House-hire of his Aids de Camp from 1st Dec. 1775 to Jan. 1784. -   33,323, 8 8
4. To Pundits, their diet and charges while employed in compiling the Code of Hindoo Laws; to charges attending the translating the Laws of Mahomed, and for the Expence of the Mahomedan Academy - - -   85,357, 11 9
5. To Budgeroes and Boats for the Governor General's use since 1781 to 18th Jan. 1784, - -   59,165, 5 9

Rupees 3,36,228, 13 5

Note. No. 2, this Article consists chiefly of Charges for Pens, Ink, Paper, Tape, &c. with Clerks Salaries,

REMARKS.

A LETTER from a Governor General of Bengal, acknowledging the private receipt of money and the application of it to his own ufe, is an object of curiofity. The fact, if not fairly and clearly accounted for, muft naturally excite fufpicion. But, if the account he gives of it be palpably defective, obfcure, and contradictory, curiofity and fufpicion will give way to other fentiments, efpecially in the minds of men, who have hitherto thought favourably of Mr. Haftings. I mean to examine his letter ftrictly, but without paffion or invective.

The firft point to be confidered is the time and circumftances, in which it was written. There may be fome merit in a voluntary and feafonable confeffion of queftionable acts. But, if it be partially made, or at a fufpicious moment, or under the apprehenfion of a difcovery, confeffion then not only forfeits all pretenfions to merit,
but

but indicates a ftate of mind enfeebled and perplexed by the confcioufnefs of guilt. This general obfervation may ferve for a clew through many myfterious paffages of Mr. Haftings's writings and conduct. His prefent letter, when written, had very much the air of a winding up not only of his government, but of his life. He fays *he has lately received more than one fevere warning to retire ;* and, if we may believe what he adds of the actual infirmities of his body and mind, his life was not likely to be a long one. It is evident at leaft that, while he was writing this letter, he did not expect to continue long in the government. In February, 1784, he had heard of the laft arrangement of the adminiftration in England, which placed the Duke of Portland and Mr. Fox at the head of affairs. He knew that the power, which had hitherto fupported him, had been obliged to give way, and that a fyftem, from which he had no protection to expect, was likely to prevail at home. Such was the opinion current in England in the fummer of 1783, and

and the only one, that could have been im-
preffed upon him at that period by all public and private advices. . Without entering
into the merits or demerits of the arrange-
ments then in contemplation for the government of India, it is of importance to remark, that one certain effect of thofe arrange-
ments, with refpect to Mr. Haftings, would
have been his immediate removal at leaft,
if it went no further. The moft favourable
event he could hope for was fimply to be
recalled. But, if an adminiftration, by
whom he thought he was condemned,
fhould be difpofed to avail themfelves of the
heavy votes of cenfure, which were drawn
up by Mr. Dundas and Sir Adam Fergufon,
and paffed the Houfe of Commons in 1782,
who could fay to what extent their inquiries
into the detail of his government might be
carried, where they would ftop, or to what
termination they might lead? In thefe circumftances, there could be no impreffion,
but that of fear, on the mind of Mr. Haftings ; and under that impreffion he muft
have acted, at the period in queftion. Many
private

private letters mention that, when he fet out on his laft expedition to Lucknow, his fpirits were funk into the loweft ftate of dejection.

Carrying this view of his fituation and reflexions into the examination of his letter, we may account for many things, which he has left unexplained.

1ft. He has received money *privately*, which, if once he were removed from the government, would probably be difcovered. The prefent confeffion therefore is extorted from him. It is imperfect as it ftands, and comes too late. Acts of this nature fhould be declared at the moment they are done. When they are acknowledged, they fhould be explained. If Mr. Haftings meant to clear his character, he fhould have told his employers, at what time he received the money, from whom, and on what account. A late and partial confeffion can have no object but to anticipate detection. A confeffion, which fpecifies no particulars, defeats the

the effect of a future discovery. Any transaction of this kind, at any period, will be covered by a previous general acknowledgement of the private receipt of money. For how can it be determined, that any particular sums, which he may hereafter happen to have received, were not included in his general confession?

2*d.* He has received money, which he is very unwilling to relinquish and afraid to conceal. To entitle him to keep it, he makes out a bill of expences against the Company, which, until this time, he had no intention of charging, and loads it with all the petty items *that he can glean from his past accounts,* and which, for twelve years together, he had totally overlooked. This he calls a debt *justly due to him,* and concludes that it will not be disputed by the Directors, since he has found out a private method of discharging it.

3*d.* Supposing him to expect a future enquiry into the transactions of his Government,
ment,

ment, nothing can be of greater moment to him than to create a general prejudice, if he can, in favour of his integrity; efpecially if the fame evidence, that proves his integrity, has a tendency to excite the compaffion of men, and to conciliate their benevolence. Mr. Haftings therefore, *in formâ pauperis*, is to be reprefented to the world as a man, who, after all his fervices, retires at laft from his great employments with a fortune hardly fufficient to furnifh him with the comforts of life; much lefs to reward him for his labours. The pains taken by his agents, to fpread and inculcate a general opinion of his poverty, are well known. But he himfelf has overacted his purpofe. Not contented with profeffing to have acquired only a moderate fortune, which in a comparative fenfe might poffibly be allowed, he threatens the Company with the injury, which their interefts fhould fuffer, *by the example of a life* (fuch as his) *doomed on its clofe to fuffer the extremities of private want, and to fink into obfcurity!*

A Man,

A Man, who pleads extreme poverty when his fortune might fairly have been affluent, and when the legiflature intended and provided that it fhould be fo, ought firft to fhew that he really is as poor as he pretends to be; and fecondly, by what means fo great an income as he has enjoyed can have been honeftly as well as compleatly expended. An appeal to the paffions before the underftanding is fatisfied, is fufpicious and premature. A plea of diftrefs, that exceeds all bounds of probability, not only deferves no credit, but argues a confufion in the judgment of the perfon who makes it. It is true that any artifice, however grofs, may deceive the multitude; but men of penetration will call Mr. Haftings to a ftricter account.

4th. The *fubftance* of this letter is not the only evidence of the diforder and perplexity, in which it appears to have been written. It is faid of Mr. Haftings that he writes Englifh with the utmoft elegance and perfpicuity. If he be not by this time,

D   a per-

a perfect mafter of compofition, undoubtedly it is not for want of practife. Yet the
expreffions he makes ufe of, on a fubject
that demanded nothing but plain language,
are for the moft part affected and intricate,
and in fome places unintelligible. To a
common eye, this circumftance proves nothing, men of deeper judgment will com-
bine it with other evidence, and with *them*
it will have its weight. The reader is re-
quefted to carry thefe general ideas along
with him through the following difcuff-
ion.

In the firft paragraph Mr. Haftings de-
clares, that he has received various fums
privately, a part of which he has heretofore
carried to the Company's account, but that
he has refolved to apply the remainder to
his own ufe, to reimburfe himfelf for fundry expences, which he had been obliged
to incur in their fervice, but which he had
hitherto omitted to charge in his public
accounts ; and he fays he does it now, becaufe *his own fortune is unequal to fo heavy
a charge.*

a charge. In the early part of a lucrative government, thefe voluntary expences were not too heavy for him; but, when he has held it long enough to accumulate a fortune, he can fupport them no longer, and now he muſt be reimburſed by the public. His poverty compels him *to glean from his paſt accounts all the little articles of expences which his inaccuracy or indifference hath over-looked.* The probable amount of his fortune ſhall be confidered in its place.

It is true, that an extraordinary occafion will fometimes juſtify a public officer in incurring an extraordinary expence. But, in every inſtance, the fact and the reaſons for it ſhould be immediately reported to his employers, that they may judge for themſelves whether fuch charges are proper, whether they ought to be allowed, and particularly, whether they ought to be continued. On this principle, neglecting to make his charge in proper time precludes him from making it at any time. A Governor, who for feveral years omits to en-

D 2

ter

ter in his public accounts any incidental expences not provided for by his eftablifh-ment, or authorized by his fuperiors, may with reafon be fufpected to have purpofely kept them out of fight during the time when his accounts might have been ex-amined, and when fuch expences might at leaft have been prohibited in future.

Mr. Haftings forefeeing that his claim might be fubject to difficulties, if he really left it to the Court of Directors, very pru-dently refolved to reimburfe himfelf. He receives money *privately*, without difcover-ing from whom, or on what account, and he pays himfelf out of it, and this he calls *a mode moft fuitable to the Company's affairs.*

In the firft place, his receiving money privately, on *any* account, is pofitively a-gainft law, and againft the very law, which created his office, and made him what he was. In a man fo trufted, difobedience is breach f truft, and the importance of the truft is the meafure of the crime.

Secondly,

Secondly, There is not a native of Bengal either willing or able to give Mr. Haſtings money, without an adequate ſervice in return of ſome ſort or other, which can only be rendered at the Company's expence. A Zemindar will readily give one lack of rupees to a Collector to be excuſed two in his rent. It reſts with Mr. Haſtings or his friends to ſhew, what poſſible motive, but a corrupt one, could engage any native to give him money privately.

Thirdly, Since Mr. Haſtings, by his own confeſſion, is in the habit of receiving money *privately*, how are the Directors to know whether he has confeſſed *all* that he had received? It is plain that he can conceal the amount of his receipts if he pleaſes. In his letter of the 16th. December 1782, he tells the Directors, that " he " could have concealed theſe tranſactions" *(viz. ſome others of the ſame ſort)* " if he had " a wrong motive, from theirs and the " public eye for ever." Receiving money againſt law is not an indifferent action in a
Governor.

Governor. If he had no *wrong* motive, what motive had he? And what was the view or expectation of the person, who gave it? Would any man of common understanding suffer his steward to receive money privately among his tenants under the pretence of paying himself *in a mode most suitable to his master's affairs?* or would he be satisfied with such an account as Mr. Hastings has given the Directors? In a trust of the lowest order, such conduct would be deemed a sufficient evidence of fraud. Much less is it to be endured in a man, in whose integrity the legislature have placed a distinguished confidence, and who, standing high himself, is looked up to as an example. The eminence of his station makes it essentially *his* duty to set a good example to those, who are under his authority and subject to his influence. Can he check in others the abuses he commits? Can he punish offences, of which he himself is guilty?

Fourthly,

Fourthly, If this *mode* of difcharging the Company's debts be *the moft fuitable to their affairs*, what are we to conclude, but that their affairs are in extreme diftrefs? A government, whofe annual revenue is ftated at four millions, cannot defray an extra expence *required to enable the Governor to execute the duties of his ftation*, unlefs he receives money *privately*. Retrenchments, œconomy, and good management, are the courfes, which every ftate ought to purfue for the recovery of its affairs. Receiving bribes to fupport extravagance cannot laft long and muft be the ruin of the government. Every man in office under Mr. Haftings might act as he has done, make ufe of the fame pretences, and plead his example for it. Finally, fuppofing the diftrefs of the Company's affairs to be a juftification of fuch practifes, it ought not to be one in Bengal, fince Mr. Haftings himfelf,* very lately affured the Directors that, " it had been the diftinguifhed lot of the " lands immediately fubject to the govern-
" ment,

* 16th December, 1783.

" ment, over which he prefided, to have
" enjoyed the clear and uninterrupted *fun-*
" *fhine* of wealth, peace, and abundance,
" and to have dealt out a portion of thefe
" bleffings to remote ftates and members
" of the Britifh dominions."—He might
have called it moonfhine with greater propriety.

Of the five accounts of difburfements now
produced by Mr. Haftings, it may be obferved
in general, that there is not one, of which the
Board at Calcutta was not as competent to
judge as himfelf; and the chief of them,
viz. for a Mahomedan academy, ought to
have been previoufly recommended to the
Court of Directors, and their fanction obtained before the fcheme was undertaken.

Lieutenant Colonel Ironfide, as Military
Secretary, had no claim to extraordinary
pay from the Company on account of his
fuperior rank, nor does it appear that he
made any. Eftablifhments are ufelefs, if
fuch precedents are admitted. On the
Britifh ftaff, the pay of Secretary to the
Commander in chief is ten fhillings a day,
and,

and, whether the duty be done by an En-
fign or Field-Officer, never varies.

The fecond account containing a charge
of nearly 15,000l. for difburfements in his
office of Governor-General, viz. hire of
clerks, ftationary, &c. &c. The only offices,
in which the Governor-General acts dif-
tinctly from the Council, are thofe of the
Perfian correfpondence and military com-
mand in Fort William. For the firft, there
is a compleat eftablifhment under the Perfian Tranflator, and a Military Secretary for
the bufinefs of the fecond, who, with all
their petty difburfements, are liberally provided for by the Company. As to ftationary, the Company fend out immenfe
quantities of it every year for the ufe of
all the public offices at Calcutta. It is not
unlikely that Mr. Haftings' accounts and
correfpondence may be voluminous; but he
has no right to load the Company with the
expence of an office for the management
of his private affairs.

E   The

The third charge for houfe-rent to his Aids de Camp will appear unbecoming as well as irregular in Mr. Haftings, if it be confidered that the Company, as a mark of perfonal refpect to him, allowed him to enjoy a houfe both in town and country rent-free, and that he accommodated himfelf with another houfe in Calcutta at their expence and without their permiffion.

No. 4. In this account, the firft article feems too pitiful to be charged by a man, who receives twenty-five thoufand pounds a year from the Company. The fecond, if proper, ought to have been provided for by the board at Calcutta. Mr. Haftings firft indulges his vanity in having it underftood that all thefe fervices are accomplifhed at his own expence, that he is the promoter of learning and patron of men of letters, and that he fcorns to carry fuch charges to the Company's account. When this fort of oftentation has anfwered its purpofe, he fuddenly turns fhort upon the Company and infifts upon their defraying the charges he has

has been put to in acquiring a reputation of generofity. It is the perfection of prudence, to be reputed bountiful and to make others pay for it.

With refpect to his Mahomedan academy, there was nothing fo very preffing in the want of it, efpecially in time of war and in the midft of public diftrefs, but that it might have waited for the approbation of the Court of Directors, on whom at that very time he was drawing bills to the a-mount of feveral millions fterling. That he may have erected a building for an academy is not unlikely, becaufe a building fuppofes a contract, and a contract makes the fortune of a contractor. But that he has done it *at his own immediate coft* is evidently untrue. He fays himfelf that *a Company's interefted note has been granted him for the reimburfement of it.* Now it cannot be faid that a man, who lends his money on a bond bearing eight per cent. intereft, is either immediately or ultimately at the expence of any work, to which the money

so lent may be applied. He has placed himself on a footing with the other creditors of the Company, who have lent their money on the same security and received the same interest for it that he does. But what are the sciences taught in the Mahomedan schools? Can he name any one Mussulman or European who has studied in this academy? Where did they study in the two years before the building was erected? What proof has he that this academy *was likely to answer the end of it's institution*, and why has he produced none? In short, who is there that ever heard of his academy before?—*The decayed remains of these schools are yet to be seen in the principal cities of Indostan!* This indeed is true. Whereever the British dominion has extended, the ruins of ancient establishments are the only traces that are left of them. The greater part of Mr. Hastings's political life has been employed in promoting wars, in the Company's name, by which India, though not conquered, has been utterly laid waste. But it seems that this academy has already contributed

tributed to extend the credit of the Company's name and to soften the prejudices excited by the rapid growth of the British dominions! The Company's name is sufficiently known in the East. There was no occasion to do any thing to extend it. But, if the universal devastation and ruin of their country have excited prejudices against us in the minds of the natives of India, of whom ninety-nine in an hundred are *Hindoos*, it may be doubted, whether they will be much softened by the institution of a *Mahomedan* academy at Calcutta. Is it already a consolation to all the nations from Cape Comorin to Surat, whose country has been the seat of war, or to the wretched inhabitants of the Carnatic who may have survived the desolation of their country, that Mr. Hastings has erected an academy at Calcutta? After carrying fire and sword into every quarter of India, where it was possible for our armies to penetrate, does he think that the institution of a school compensates for all the havock he has made, or repairs all the mischief he has done?—Absurdity is not incompatible with cunning. A man, who

who is fure of his audience, may hold what language he thinks fit.

Mr. Haftings fays *it was not poffible for him to have been influenced, in incurring thefe expences, by any purpofe of his own intereft.* The truth of this propofition is not felf-evident ; and, if it were, it would be no reafon for carrying them to the Company's account. Who can determine that there is no profit on expenditures made without authority, for which he reimburfes himfelf, and for which no vouchers are produced ? As to his motive for doing what he had no fort of right to do, whether it was pride, or vanity, or oftentation, is immaterial. He, who thinks fuch a queftion worth difcuffing, muft be paffionately fond of talking of himfelf.

On the three articles, of which the account of No. 4 is compofed, one general remark occurs. He begins his letter with afferting, that the fums, which he had had *occafion to difburfe* were *for fervices required to enable him to execute the duties of his ftation.* But

But how the entertainment of learned Muf-
fulmen, or the inftitution of an academy
have been neceffary for that purpofe, is a
myftery, which he has prudently aban-
doned to the conjectures of the Court of
Directors.

He *candidly confeffes that, when he firft
engaged both in this and the preceding expences, he had no intention of carrying it to
the account of the Company. At that time he
was improvident for himfelf.* At *that* time,
*the exercife of his faculties was undifturbed.
He confined all his regards to his public character, and reckoned on a fund of years for its
duration.* If, by this laft myfterious ex-
preffion, it be meant that he depended on
continuing many years in office, his expectation has not been difappointed. He
has no right to fay or infinuate, that he
has not been allowed fufficient time to
provide for the eftablifhment of his fortune
notwithftanding the careleffnefs and im-
providence, with which he at firft neglec-
ted *his profpects of futurity.* Suppofing this
to

to be his meaning, the affertion is intelligible, though not true. The words, in which he involves it, exprefs nothing but nonfenfe.

But now, it feems, all the preceding circumftances are reverfed. The *infirmities of life have fince fucceeded. His bodily ftrength* is impaired, and the *powers of mind he once poffeffed* decay along with it. If it be of any ufe to him to prove, that he has loft his underftanding, the prefent letter may anfwer his purpofe. He has even loft his ftyle, and cannot write plain Englifh. Who ever heard of a man's *difcharging the hard viciffitudes of his ftation*, or calling the latter part of his own life his *profpects of futurity ?* or of *an interefted note* for a bond bearing intereft ? Taking every thing for granted that he has faid of himfelf, let us fee what conclufion he has drawn from the premifes. Why, *this change in his condition compels him to depart from that liberal plan, which he originally adopted.* Did he expect to be immortal, or to continue in the government

to

to the end of his life, or that age would *not* affect his health, or impair his faculties ? Difappointed in his expectations, whatever they were, he now finds himfe f *compelled* to claim from the *juftice* of the Directors the difcharge of *a debt*. It is not an equitable appeal to their generofity but the pofitive demand of a debt ftrictly due to him. To gratify his own pride (for pride he admits) and without any intention of charging the Company with fuch expences, he gives falaries to learned men, tranflates a book, and founds an academy. In procefs of time, he finds his health and faculties fo much impaired, that he is *compelled* to infift on being reimburfed, and he demands it as his right. Such is the foundation of his claim and immediate motive for making it. A debt, fo claimed, ought to be proved. Mr. Haftings contents himfelf with faying, *I can, with the moft fcrupulous integrity, aver it to be juftly my due.* But in truth whether his appeal be to their juftice or their generofity, is of no fort of moment, where he has previoufly *refolved to reimburfe himfelf*

F   whether

whether the Directors approve of it or not.

He suppofes *it may be objected that the allowance of thefe demands would furnifh a precedent for others, of the like kind.* If the debt be juftly due to him, the payment of it can furnifh no precedent injurious to the Company. Debts, juftly due, muft at all times be paid, whether with or without a precedent. But, fuppofing thefe claims of his to be fuch, as the Directors are at liberty to deny if they think proper, the objection then is a ftrong one, and he has not anfwered it. It is a dangerous precedent indeed, to fuffer any man in a public truft to run up a private bill without the confent or knowledge of his employers, and at the end of twelve years to infift upon their paying it. But this it feems is *not* dangerous; or, if it be, *their intereft would fuffer lefs by the precedent than by a fingle example of a life fpent in the accumulation of crores for their benefit, and doomed in its clofe to fuffer the extremitie. of private want and fink in obfcurity!*

fcurity! This indeed is a melancholy conclufion, and poffibly might make an impreffion on the benevolent hearts of the Directors, if he had not before affured them
(in his letter of the 20th of January 1782)
that his office had at leaft enabled him to lay up
a provifion with which he could be contented
in a more humble ftation; and if he had not,
in another letter dated 11th November
1773, declared, that *a very few years poffeffion*
of the government would undoubtedly enable him
to retire with a fortune amply fitted to the mea-
*fure of his defires.** If it fhould now appear
that Mr. Haftings's fervices and circumftances are fuch as he defcribes them, his
neceffities may deferve to be confidered.
That queftion is material, and fhall be exa-
mined by itfelf.

He concludes his account with a charge
of about fix thoufand pounds fterling for
boats provided by him for his own ufe. If
his predeceffors have always had an eftablifh-

---

* Vide Appendix to 5th Report of Sec. Com.
No. 5.

ment

ment of this kind provided for them, he ought to have been contented with it. The indulgence of perfonal vanity is endlefs, when others are to pay for it. But it feems thefe boats are *fuperior in convenience and elegance to any that Mr. Haftings has yet feen.* The Proprietors of India ftock will be happy to hear it. Their fervant affures them that his boats have been *furnifhed with a coft, which would not be credited by thofe, who have feen the fubjects of it.* Mr. Haftings's friends have often boafted the fimplicity of his manners, and he himfelf profeffes to carry it even to *humility.* In one of his narratives, he fays, " the Raja of Benares left " his capital with a large retinue; but, " hearing that I came unattended, he dif- " miffed his followers and met me with a " ftate as *humble* as mine."

But, alas! the infirmities of life have fucceeded, and his faculties are impaired by them!

Thefe

These demands, put together, form an object by no means inconfiderable. Under five heads only, the amount of what he calls *little articles of expence gleaned from his paft accounts* is current rupees 3.36.220; or very nearly thirty four thoufand pounds fterling.

The probable fituation of his fortune remains to be confidered. They, who have hitherto infifted moft on the moderate amount of it, have at all times allowed him to poffefs about feventy or eighty thoufand pounds, which they truly afferted was a fmall fortune for a man fo long in the government of Bengal, and fo much longer in lucrative employments. All the principal offices in the Company's fervice are lucrative. In the prefent letter, Mr. Haftings reduces himfelf to pofitive and abfolute beggary, though his life has been *fpent in the accumulation of crores* for the Company. The fecond part of this propofition is juft as true as the firft. If fo many millions have been accumulated, where are they ?

Since

Since the year 1777 he has drawn upon the
Directors for many millions fterling and incurred a heavy bonded debt in Bengal. In
the fame period, bills have been drawn and
debts incurred to the amount of feveral
millions more at Fort St. George and Bombay, and properly the whole ought to be
placed to the account of Mr. Haftings the
contriver and author of the Maratta war.
A calculation of thefe accumulations is ftated in the Appendix.

He now wifhes it to be underftood that,
while he was accumulating fo many millions for the Company, he has totally neg-
lected his private fortune. Whether he did
or not, the fact is, that his fortune was amply provided for by his appointments. Let
it be fuppofed for a moment, that he had
no fhare in the bounty of Coffim Ally
Cawn, who is pretty well known to have
diftributed twenty lacks of rupees among
fome perfons of Mr. Haftings's acquain-
tance ; that he got nothing by the depofition
of Meer Jaffier in 1760, or that he loft it
again

again in a commercial fpeculation; that he faved nothing while he was fecond in council at Madrafs, and in fhort that he was not worth a fhilling when he was appointed to the government of Bengal. Since that time, twelve years and a half have elapfed, in which his avowed receipts and vifible. expences, being eftimated and compared, will fhew what he is or ought to be worth at prefent. With refpect to the annexed ftatements of the credit due to them, it is to be obferved

1ſt. That he is not charged with any receipts beyond his falary, except a lack and a half of rupees received from *Munny Begum*, which never was difputed.

2d. That his falary, as limited by Act of Parliament in 1773, to £.25,000 was always reckoned to be lefs that the profits of his place as they ftood before.

3d. That houfe rent, the principal article of expence in Bengal, was defrayed
for

for him. He had three houfes (two in Calcutta and one in the country) rented, furnifhed, and kept in repair by the Company;
who are alfo at the charge of the general
entertainments, to which the Governor in-
vites the fettlement three or four times a
year. So that, out of his great falary, he had
literally nothing to provide for but his table,
equipage, private fervants, and perfonal expences. In thefe, by all accounts, there was
no appearance of extravagance. Eight thoufand current rupees a month is a liberal allowance for them. It would be difficult to
fhew how they could poffibly amount to that
fum.

4th. The falaries of the Governor and
Council are paid to them in Bengal, at one
fhilling and nine pence half-penny the current rupee; but, by an eftablifhed indulgence of the Company to their fervants,
when they remit their fortunes back again
by bills on the Directors, the treafury at
Fort William receives the current rupee at
two fhillings and a penny and fometimes
higher, which gives them a profit of three
pence

pence halfpenny on every rupee fo remitted.

5th. The firft ftatement fuppofes him
not to have improved his growing capital,
by putting any part of it out at lawful intereft.—The fecond fuppofes him to have
improved his favings at fimple intereft only.
The third fuppofes him to have improved
them, as he might fairly and honeftly have
done, at compound intereft. In the firft
cafe his prefent fortune ought to be

$$£261,265.$$

In the *2d.* ——£303,418, 3.
In the *3d.* ——£425,226, 4.

Mr. Haftings, if he has availed himfelf of
all thefe advantages except the prefent from
Munny Begum, has done nothing that he
was not fairly intitled to do. There may
be objections to thefe eftimates, but none
that will materially reduce the total. Much
lefs can any deductions be reafonably made

from

from the amount, that will leave him in danger of *suffering the extremities of private want*. For any thing that appears to the contrary to the public eye, a medium of the three totals, viz. £329,969. 15s. 8d. ought to be taken for a fair and moderate eſtimate of his actual fortune. If not, what has he done with it? It is true that he talks of his inaccuracy, and would willingly be thought a man careleſs about money mat-ters. But we have the evidence of the con-trary before us. He has kept an exact ac-count of the minuteſt articles of expence, and even of his charities.

There is another way of eſtimating his fortune, which would encreaſe it conſidera-bly; that is, if he were to be debited with the ſums which he has been accuſed of re-ceiving, or even with thoſe which he has acknowledged.

In March 1775 he was charged by the unfortunate Raja Nandcomar with the

receipt

receipt of various fums paid to him by the Raja to the amount of funaut rupees 3,54,105, or about £36,000. The accufer not only fpecified all manner of particulars, but came forward, at every poffible perfonal hazard, to make good his charge. If it was falfe, it was at once the moft daring and abfurd falfehood that ever was attempted. *Dolus in generalibus verfatur*—Falfehood never defcends to particulars. The Raja however was inftantly hanged, and his charge, whether true or falfe, muft be difmiffed out of this account. At prefent, it is not meant to infift on any thing, but what Mr. Haftings himfelf has acknowledged. In his letter to the Directors dated 22d of May 1782, but not difpatched from Calcutta until the 16th of December following, he gives them an account of *various fums occafionally converted to the Company's property through his means,* amounting at that time to nineteen lack and a half of current rupees, or £195,000, all which, he fays, he has carried to the Company's credit. But, of

G 2   this

this fum, he admits that he had taken their bonds at eight per cent. for four lacks and fix thoufand rupees, and that he had credit in the account of depofits in the Company's treafury for 2,38,715 rupees more, which he might have called for when he would, and received on demand. If the money was their own, he had no right to take a fecurity for it. He could have no right to lend them their own money at intereft. Or,—fuppofing it poffible to invent a pretence, for this courfe of proceeding, or admitting, as he fays, that he *poffibly acted without any ftudied defign which his memory could at that diftance of time verify*, the bonds ought to have been cancelled long ago, which it is not known that he has done. In his poffeffion, they are a legal fecurity to him and his heirs, and as long as they exift make part of his fortune. The remaining thirteen lacks are faid to be expended in Durbar charges, which confift chiefly of bounties and prefents made by Government and of fecret fervices only

known

known to the Governor. Of thefe no judgment can be formed unlefs the particulars
were produced.

It is to be prefumed that, when Mr.
Haftings' Letter and the preceding Remarks upon it are coolly and impartially
confidered, no rational being can believe,
that he is really in that ftate of penury
and diftrefs, which he defcribes. There
is no degree of human credulity, that will
reach to fuch a belief. And yet it may
poffibly be true that his fortune is not
fo confiderable as apparently it ought to
be. He may have appropriated large
fums to fervices, not proper to be explained, that is, to the fupport of his
intereft in England. On that prefumption, his poverty becomes criminal in
whatever degree the fuppofition makes
it credible. If he has wafted his fortune
to obtain protection, the inference is
plain,—that his actions required intereft
and favour to protect them, and that
his

his poverty arifes from his fuccefs in corrupting the integrity of perfons whofe truft and ftation gave them power to fupport him.

F I N I S.

APPENDIX, No. I.

Extract of a letter from Warren Haftings, Efq. to the Court of Directors, dated 22d of May, 1782, but not difpatched until the 16th of December following.

" WHY thefe fums were taken by me;
" why they were, except the fecond, *quietly*
" transferred to the Company's ufe; why
" bonds were taken for the firft, and not
" for the reft, might, were this matter to
" be expofed to the view of the Public,
" furnifh a variety of conjectures to which
" it would be of little ufe to reply. Were
" your Honourable Court to queftion me
" on thefe points, I would anfwer, that
" the fums were taken for the Company's
" benefit, at times in which the Company
" very much needed them; that I either

H   " chofe

APPENDIX.

" chose to conceal the first receipts from
" the public curiosity, by receiving bonds
" for the amount; or possibly acted *with-*
" *out any studied design* which my memory
" could *at this distance of time* verify; and
" that I did not think it worth my care to
" observe the same means with the rest.
" I trust, Honourable Sirs, to your breasts
" for a candid interpretation of my actions,
" and assume the freedom to add, that I
" think myself, *on such a subject*, and on
" such an occasion, entitled to it."

---

*Copy of a Letter from Mr. Hastings to the
Court of Directors, dated 16th December,
1782.*

" Honourable Sirs,

"THE dispatch of the Lively having been
" protracted, by various causes, from time
" to time, the accompanying address, which
" was originally designed and prepared for
" that dispatch, (no other conveyance since
" occuring) has of course been thus long
" detained.

APPENDIX.

" detained. The delay is of no public con-
" fequence ; but it has produced a fitua-
" tion, which, with refpect to myfelf, I
" regard as unfortunate, becaufe it expofes
" me to the meaneft imputation, from the
" occafion, which the late Parliamentary
" enquires have fince furnifhed, but which
" were unknown when my letter was
" written, and written in the neceffary con-
" fequence of a promife, made to that effect
" in a former letter to your Honourable
" Committee, dated 20th January laft.
" However, to preclude the poffibility of
" fuch reflections from affecting me, I
" have defired Mr. Larkins, who was
" privy to the whole tranfaction, to affix
" to the letter his affidavit of the date in
" which it was written. I own I feel moft
" fenfibly the mortification of being re-
" duced to the neceffity of ufing fuch pre-
" cautions to guard my reputation from
" difhonour. If I had, *at any time,* pof-
" feffed that degree of confidence from my
" immediate employers, which they never
" withheld from the *meaneft* of my pre-
H 2 deceffors,

" deceffors, I fhould have difdained to ufe
" thefe attentions. How I have drawn on
" me a different treatment I know not; it
" is fufficient that I have not merited it :
" and in the courfe of a fervice of thirty-
" two years, and ten of thefe employed in
" maintaining the powers and difcharging
" the duties of the firft office of the Britifh
" Government in India, that Honourable
" Court ought to know whether I poffefs
" the integrity and honour, which are the
" firft requifites of fuch a ftation. If I
" wanted thefe, they have afforded me but
" too powerful incentives to fupprefs the
" information, which I now convey to
" them through you ; and to appropriate
" to my own ufe the fums, which I have
" already paffed to their credit, by the un-
" worthy, and pardon me if I add danger-
" ous reflections which they have paffed
" upon me, for the firft communication of
" this kind ; and *your own experience* will
" fuggeft to *you*, that there are perfons,
" who would profit by fuch a warning.

" Upon

" Upon the whole of thefe tranfaĉtions,
" which to you, who are accuftomed to
" view bufinefs in an official and regular
" light, may appear unprecedented, if not
" improper, I have but a few fhort remarks
" to fuggeft to your confideration. If I
" appear in any unfavourable light by thefe
" tranfaĉtions, I refign the common and
" legal fecurity of thofe who commit
" crimes, or errors. I am ready to anfwer
" every particular queftion, that may be
" put againft myfelf, upon honour, or up-
" on oath.

" The fources, from which thefe reliefs
" to the public fervice have come, would
" never have yielded them to the Company
" publickly; and the exigencies of your
" fervice (exigencies created by the ex-
" pofition of your affairs and faĉtion in
" your Councils) required thofe fupplies.

" I could have concealed them, had I a
" wrong motive, from yours and the public
" eye for ever; and I know that the dif-
" ficulties,

" ficulties, to which a fpirit of injuftice may
" fubject me, for my candour and avowal,
" are greater than any poffible incon-
" venience that could have attended the
" concealment, except the diffatisfaction of
" my own mind. Thefe difficulties are
" but a few of thofe, which I have fuffered
" in your fervice. The applaufe of my
" own breaft is my fureft reward, and was
" the fupport of my mind in meeting
" them ; your applaufe and that of my
" country, are my next wifh in life.

I have the Honour to be, &c.

WARREN HASTINGS."

N.B. It is very material to obferve that Mr.
Haftings, who, as he himfelf affirms, " has
" *at no time* poffeffed that degree of con-
" fidence from his immediate employers,
" which they never withheld from the
" *meaneft* of his predeceffors," has neverthe-
lefs received the unanimous thanks of thofe
immediate employers, viz. the Court of
Directors, for his long, able, and faithful
fervices,

fervices. It feems alfo very neceffary that Mr. Haftings fhould ftate to the Company, whom it is that he means to defcribe by the words " *the meaneft of his predeceffors*," was it Governor Cartier, or Mr. Verelft, or Mr. Van Sittart, or does he mean the late Lord Clive?

APPENDIX No. II.

Extracts from the eleventh Report of the Select Committee, on the Subject of the preceding Letters.

" WHATEVER the caufe of thefe new
" difcoveries *(made by Mr. Haftings)* might
" have been, at the time of fending them,
" the fact of the Parliamentary enquiry
" was publickly known, for, in his letter
" of the 15th of December, 1782, he ex-
" prefsly mentions his fears, that thofe
" Parlia-

" Parliamentary enquiries might be thought
" to have extorted from him the con-
" feffions which he had made.

" He fays that in all the long period of
" his fervice, he has almoft unremittedly
" wanted the fupport, which all his pre-
" deceffors had enjoyed from their con-
" ftituents. From mine *(fays be)* I have
" received nothing but *reproach, hard epi-*
" *thets and indignities,* inftead of rewards
" and encouragement."

What Mr. Haftings fays further on this
fubject, is no lefs worthy of attention; viz.
that he could have concealed thefe tranfactions,
if he had a wrong motive, from theirs and the
public eye for ever. It is undoubtedly true
that, whether the obfervation be applicable to the particular cafe or not, practifes
of this corrupt nature are extremely difficult of detection any where, but efpecially in India. But all reftraints upon that
grand fundamental abufe of prefents is gone
for ever, if the fervants of the Company
                                        can

can derive fafety from a defiance of the law, when they can no longer hope to fcreen themfelves by an evafion of it. All hope of reformation is at an end, if, confiding in the force of a faction among Directors or Proprietors, to bear them out, and poffibly to vote them the fruit of their crimes as a reward of their difcovery, they find that their bold avowal of their offences is not only to produce indemnity, but to be rated for merit. If once a prefumption is admitted, that wherever fomething is divulged, nothing is hid, the difcovering of one offence may become the certain means of concealing a multitude of others. The contrivance is eafy and trivial, and lies open to the meaneft proficient in this kind of art: it will not only become an effectual cover to fuch practices, but will tend infinitely to increafe them. In that cafe, fums of money will be taken for the purpofe of difcovery and making merit with the Company; and other fums will be taken for the private advantage of the receiver.

I   *Extract*

APPENDIX.

Extract from the Eleventh Report, page 13.

H E profeffes not to be certain of the motives, by which he was himfelf actuated in fo extraordinary a concealment, and in the ufe of fuch extraordinary means to effect it : And, as if the acts in queftion were thofe of an abfolute ftranger, and not his own, he gives various loofe conjectures concerning the motive to them. He even fuppofes, in taking prefents contrary to law, and in taking bonds for them as his own, contrary to what he admits to be truth and fact, that he might have acted without any diftinct motive at all, or at leaft fuch as his memory could reach at that diftance of time. That immenfe diftance, in the faintnefs of which, his recollection is fo compleatly loft, as to fet him gueffing at his motives for his own conduct, was from the fifteenth of January, 1781, when the bonds at his own requeft were given, to the

the date of this letter which is the 22d May, 1782, that is to fay, about one year and four months. As to the other fums, for which no bond was taken, the ground for the difference in his explana-tion is ftill more extraordinary; he fays, " I did not think it worth my care to ob-" ferve the fame means with the *reft*."

The reft of thefe fums, which were not worth his care, are ftated in his account to be greater than thofe he was fo folicitous (for fome reafon which he cannot guefs) to cover under bonds. Thefe fums amount to near 53,000l. whereas the others did not much exceed 40,000l.

APPEN-

STATEMENT, No. 1.

Without Interest.

Amount of Salary received in
Bengal from April 1772 to
December 1784, is twelve
Years and nine Months at
£25,000 *per Annum*, and one
Shilling and nine-pence half-
penny per current Rupee, is

C. Rs. 35,58,142

Received from Munny Begum - 1,74,000

37,32,142

DEDUCT

Amount of Expences at 8000 *crs.*
per Month for twelve Years
nine Months, is - - - - - 12,24,000

Remains current Rupees - 25,08,142

Which at two Shillings and one
penny per current Rupee is £261,265

APPENDIX.

STATEMENT, No. 2.

With simple Interest.

Allowance of £25,000 *per Annum* received
in Bengal at 1s. 9d. ¼ per current Rupee
is - - - - - - *Crs.* 279,070

Deduct 8000 Rupees per Month
for Expences - - - - 96,000

Remains annual Savings *Crs.* 183,070

Of this annual Refidue, allow one half to
be remitted to Europe, which at *5 per
Cent.* fimple Interest has increafed, viz.
Crs. 183,070—half is 91,535—remitted
at 2s. 1d. *per. Crs.* is £9534, 18s. for
ten Years - - - - £95,349

Ten Years Interest at *5 per C.* is 4767 5

£100,116 5

Add the two firft Years Refidue on which
no Interest is calculated - - 19069 16

Ditto laft 9 Months allowances, d°.
deducting 9 Months expences 19450

138,636 1

The other half *(Crs. 91535)* remained in
Bengal at 10 *per Cent.* Interest —eleven
Years Principal is - - - 1006,885

(Crs. 91535) eleven Years
Interest at 10 *per Cent.* - 100,688 8

Crs. 11,07,573 8

Add one Year's Refidue
without Interest - - 91,535

11,99,108 8

which at 2s. 1d. *per Crs.* is 1,24,907 2

Munny Begums 174000 *Crs.* for 12 Years
at 10 *per Cent. per Ann.* 208800 is 3,82,800
which at 2s. 6d. per current Rupee is 39,875

£3,03,418 3 0

APPENDIX.

STATEMENT, No. 3.

Allowance of £25,000 *per Annum* received
in Bengal at 1s. 9d. ½ per current Rupee
is - - - - - - - - Crs. 279,070
Deduct 8000 Rupees per Month
for Expences · - - - - 96,000
Remains annual Savings   Crs. 183,070
Of this annual Refidue, allow one half to
be remitted to Europe, which at *5 per
Cent.* compound Intereſt has increaſed,
viz. Crs. 183,070—half is 91535 re-
mitted at 2s. 1d. *per Crs.* is £9534, 18s.
Ten Years is - - - - £95,349   0
Ten Years compound Intereſt
at *5 per Cent.* is - - - 30576   5
                              £125925   5
Add two Years and a half Re-
fidue, without Intereſt - 19069 16
And laſt 9 Months allowance d° 19450   6
                                   ———— 164445 7
The other half *(Crs. 91535)* remained in
Bengal at 10 *per Cent.* Intereſt—eleven
Years Principal is *Crs.* 10,06,885
Eleven Years compound
Intereſt at 10 *per Cent.* 8,58,989 14 9
                              18,65,874 14 9
Add one Year's Refidue without
Intereſt - - - 91,535
                    Crs. 19,57,409 14 9
which, at 2s. 1d. per current Rupee is   203896 17
Munny Begums - Crs. 174,000
at 10 *per Cent. per Ann.*
compound Intereſt for
twelve Years is - - 372,086   7 6
                          Crs. 5,46,086   7 6
which at 2s. 1d. per current Rupee is   56884   0

                                            £425226   4

Statement of the Crores of Rupees, or Millions Sterling, accumulated by Mr. Haftings, for the Benefit of the Eaft-India Company.

Curr^r. Rup^s.

Balance in the Treafury of Bengal at the commencement of the Maratta war, as ftated by Mr. Haftings himfelf in his minute of 10th Auguft, 1778 - - - 2,35,66,000

Cheyte Sing—his extra-contribution - - - - - - - 10,16,000

Drafts on the Court of Directors from the different ·Prefidencies fince the commencement of the Marratta war, computed moderately at fix millions fterling - - 600,00,000

Money borrowed upon bond at 8 and 9 *per Cent.* intereft at the three Prefidencies 515,99,910

Arrears due at the feveral Prefidencies - - - - - - - 381,60,270

Carried over, Curr^t. Rup^s. 1743,42,180

Brought over, Curr. Rup. 1743,42,180

*Orders on the Treasury of
Fort William unpaid, by
the latest accounts - - - -   116,58,891

Total—Current Rupees   1860,01,071

That is—Eighteen millions, six hundred thousand pounds sterling.

" N. B. * No similar accounts of Orders on the Treasuries of Fort St. George and Bombay have been received by the Court of Directors, and therefore cannot be inserted in this Statement, though the amount must be considerable."

It is material to observe that, besides the expenditure of these extraordinary supplies, all the current revenues of Bengal in the same period amounting, *communibus annis*, to four million sterling a year, have been absorbed; and that whereas, in the year 1776, there was a clear surplus of revenue (exclusive of the produce of any monopoly of salt or opium, of current rupees 129,91,547 applicable to the provision of

an

an inveftment, or to any other purpofe the Court of Directors might think fit,—The expences, by Mr. Haftings's means, have fince that time been raifed to fuch an amount that they greatly exceed the refources, as the following ftatement will fhew.

By the Bengal eftimates it appears that, in the three years ending the 1ft May 1786, the difburfements exceed the refources as follows,

1ft year ending May 1784 by cur. rupees 56,21,690
2d ———— ———— May 1785 ———— ——— 149,01,433
3d ——.———— May 1786 ——,—— —— 116,46,715

It follows therefore that, if the furplus of 1776 be added to the deficiency of 1786, there will appear and does exift a failure in the annual refources of Bengal compared with its expences, to the amount of current rupees 246,38,262. In other words, the Company's income in Bengal, compared with their expences, was better in the year 1776 than it is in the year 1786, by above two millions, four hundred and fixty three thoufand pounds fterling *per annum.*

K   *Ex-*

APPENDIX, No. V.

Extract of a Letter from Warren Haſtings, Eſq. to William Devaynes, Eſq. dated the 11th of July, 1785.

" ALTHOUGH I am firmly perſuaded,
" that theſe were my ſentiments on the
" occaſion, yet I will not affirm that they
" were. Though I feel their impreſſion,
" as the remains of a ſeries of thoughts re-
" tained on my memory, I am not certain
" that they may not have been produced by
" ſubſequent reflection on the principal
" fact, combining with it the probable mo-
" tive of it. Of this I am certain, that it
" was my deſign to have concealed the
" receipt of all the ſums, except the ſecond,
" even from the knowledge of the Court
" of Directors. They had anſwered my
" purpoſe of public utility, and I had al-
" moſt totally diſmiſſed them from my
                                          " re-

" remembrance. But when fortune threw
" a fum in my way of a magnitude *which*
" *could not be concealed*, and the peculiar
" delicacy of my fituation, at the time in
" which I received it, made me more cir-
" cumfpect of appearances, I chofe to ap-
" prife my employers of it."

E R R A T A.

Page 1, *read*, In a mode the moſt ſuitable to the ſituation of your affairs.

Page 15, line 6, *inſtead of* happen, *read* appear.

Page 42, line the laſt ; *read* Nuncomar.

www.ingramcontent.com/pod-product-compliance
Lightning Source LLC
Chambersburg PA
CBHW030022030726
47499CB00008B/3087